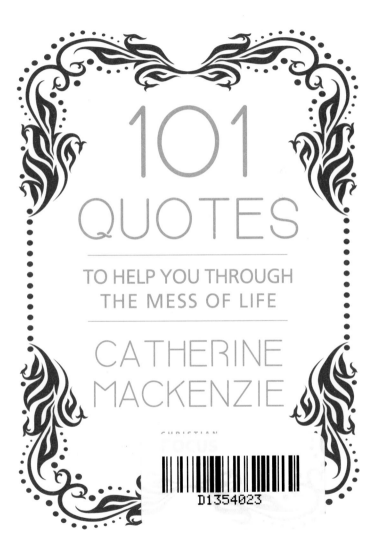

101

QUOTES

TO HELP YOU THROUGH
THE MESS OF LIFE

CATHERINE
MACKENZIE

CHRISTIAN
FOCUS

D1354023

Scripture quotations taken from the HOLY BIBLE, NEW INTERNATIONAL VERSION®, *NIV®* Copyright © 1973, 1978, 1984, 2011 by Biblica, Inc.™ Used by permission. All rights reserved worldwide.

Scripture quotations marked *ESV* are from *The Holy Bible, English Standard Versio*n, copyright © 2001 by Crossway Bibles, a publishing ministry of Good News Publishers. Used by permission. All rights reserved. *ESV Text Edition: 2011*.

10 9 8 7 6 5 4 3 2 1

Copyright © Catherine MacKenzie 2019

ISBN 978-1-5271-0381-8

First published in 2019

by Christian Focus Publications Ltd,
Geanies House, Fearn, Ross-shire
IV20 1TW, Scotland
www.christianfocus.com

Designed and typeset by: Pete Barnsley (Creativehoot.com)

Printed and bound by Bell & Bain, Glasgow

All rights reserved. No part of this publication may be reproduced, stored in a retrieval system, or transmitted, in any form, by any means, electronic, mechanical, photocopying, recording or otherwise without the prior permission of the publisher or a licence permitting restricted copying. In the U.K. such licences are issued by the Copyright Licensing Agency, Saffron House, 6-10 Kirby Street, London, EC1 8TS. www.cla.co.uk

CONTENTS

WORK,
CALLING,
LIFE

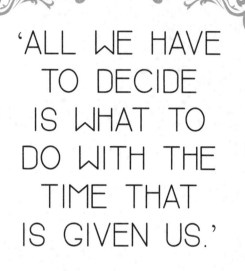

'ALL WE HAVE
TO DECIDE
IS WHAT TO
DO WITH THE
TIME THAT
IS GIVEN US.'

J.R.R. Tolkien

Teach us to number our days, that
we may gain a heart of wisdom.

(Psalm 90:12)

'OUR HIGH AND PRIVILEGED CALLING IS TO DO THE WILL OF GOD IN THE POWER OF GOD FOR THE GLORY OF GOD.'

J. I. Packer

Jesus said to her, 'Did I not tell you that if you believed you would see the glory of God?'

(John 11:40 ESV)

'WE HAVE DIFFERENT FORMS ASSIGNED TO US IN THE SCHOOL OF LIFE, DIFFERENT GIFTS IMPARTED. ALL IS NOT ATTRACTIVE THAT IS GOOD. IRON IS USEFUL, THOUGH IT DOES NOT SPARKLE LIKE THE DIAMOND. GOLD HAS NOT THE FRAGRANCE OF A FLOWER. SO DIFFERENT PERSONS HAVE VARIOUS MODES OF EXCELLENCE, AND WE MUST HAVE AN EYE TO ALL.'

William Wilberforce

The eye cannot say to the hand, 'I have no need of you,' nor again the head to the feet, 'I have no need of you.' On the contrary, the parts of the body that seem to be weaker are indispensable.

(1 Corinthians 12:21-22 ESV)

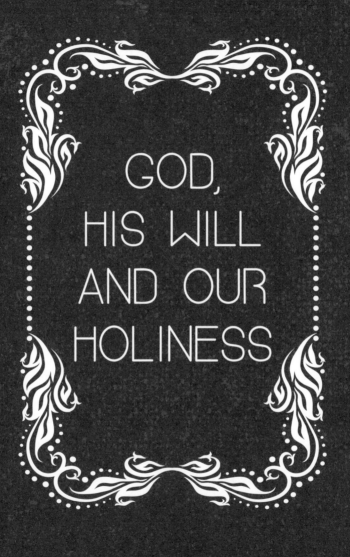

GOD,
HIS WILL
AND OUR
HOLINESS

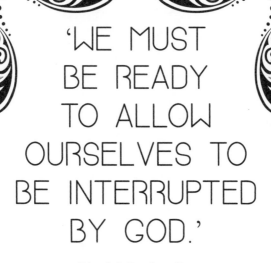

4

'WE MUST
BE READY
TO ALLOW
OURSELVES TO
BE INTERRUPTED
BY GOD.'

Dietrich Bonhoeffer

The LORD brings the counsel of
the nations to nothing; he
frustrates the plans of the peoples.

(Psalm 33:10 ESV)

'EACH ONE OF US IS GOD'S SPECIAL WORK OF ART. THROUGH US, HE TEACHES AND INSPIRES, DELIGHTS AND ENCOURAGES, INFORMS AND UPLIFTS ALL THOSE WHO VIEW OUR LIVES.'

Joni Eareckson Tada

Who is like you, O LORD, among the gods?
Who is like you, majestic in holiness,
awesome in glorious deeds, doing wonders?

(Exodus 15:11 ESV)

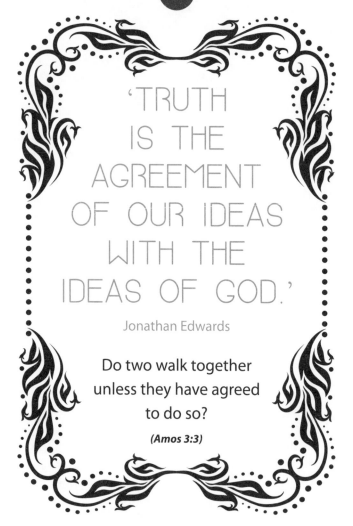

6

'TRUTH
IS THE
AGREEMENT
OF OUR IDEAS
WITH THE
IDEAS OF GOD.'

Jonathan Edwards

Do two walk together
unless they have agreed
to do so?

(Amos 3:3)

GOD, HIS WILL AND OUR HOLINESS

'HE, I KNOW, IS ABLE TO CARRY OUT HIS WILL, AND HIS WILL IS MINE. IT MAKES NO MATTER WHERE HE PLACES ME, OR HOW. THAT IS RATHER FOR HIM TO CONSIDER THAN FOR ME; FOR IN THE EASIEST POSITION HE MUST GIVE ME HIS GRACE, AND IN THE MOST DIFFICULT HIS GRACE IS SUFFICIENT.'

Hudson Taylor

Now I commit you to God and to the word of his grace, which can build you up and give you an inheritance among all those who are sanctified.

(Acts 20:32)

'OF ALL THE KNOWLEDGE THAT WE CAN EVER OBTAIN, THE KNOWLEDGE OF GOD, AND THE KNOWLEDGE OF OURSELVES, ARE THE MOST IMPORTANT.'

Jonathan Edwards

The fear of the LORD is the beginning of knowledge, but fools despise wisdom and instruction.

(Proverbs 1:7)

'BE KILLING SIN OR IT WILL BE KILLING YOU.'

John Owen

All wrongdoing is sin, and there is sin that does not lead to death.

(1 John 5:17)

SUFFERING
AND
TRUST

'IT IS GREAT TO BE
FACED WITH THE
IMPOSSIBLE, FOR
NOTHING IS IMPOSSIBLE
IF ONE IS MEANT TO
DO IT. WISDOM WILL
BE GIVEN, AND
STRENGTH. WHEN
THE LORD LEADS, HE
ALWAYS STRENGTHENS.'

Amy Carmichael

Jesus looked at them and said,
'With man this is impossible, but
with God all things are possible.'

(Matthew 19:26)

'ACCEPT YOUR LONELINESS.
IT IS ONE STAGE, AND ONLY
ONE STAGE, ON A JOURNEY
THAT BRINGS YOU TO GOD.
IT WILL NOT ALWAYS LAST.
OFFER UP YOUR LONELINESS
TO GOD, AS THE LITTLE BOY
OFFERED TO JESUS HIS FIVE
LOAVES AND TWO FISHES. GOD
CAN TRANSFORM IT FOR THE
GOOD OF OTHERS.'

Elisabeth Elliot

A new command I give you: Love one another.
As I have loved you, so you must love one
another. By this everyone will know that you
are my disciples, if you love one another.

(John 13:34-35)

  SUFFERING AND TRUST

'WORRY IS AN OLD MAN WITH BENDED HEAD, CARRYING A LOAD OF FEATHERS WHICH HE THINKS ARE LEAD.'

Corrie ten Boom

Therefore I tell you, do not worry about your life, what you will eat or drink; or about your body, what you will wear. Is not life more than food, and the body more than clothes?

(Matthew 6:25)

'THE WEAKER WE FEEL, THE HARDER WE LEAN. AND THE HARDER WE LEAN, THE STRONGER WE GROW SPIRITUALLY, EVEN WHILE OUR BODIES WASTE AWAY.'

J. I. Packer

Trust in the LORD with all your heart
    and lean not on your own understanding;
in all your ways submit to him,
    and he will make your paths straight.

(Proverbs 3:5-6)

  SUFFERING AND TRUST

'IF THE LORD
BE WITH US, WE HAVE
NO CAUSE OF FEAR.
HIS EYE IS UPON US,
HIS ARM OVER US, HIS
EAR OPEN TO OUR
PRAYER - HIS GRACE
SUFFICIENT, HIS PROMISE
UNCHANGEABLE.'

John Newton

What, then, shall we say in response to these things? If God is for us, who can be against us?

(Romans 8:31)

'MY WHEELCHAIR WAS THE KEY TO SEEING ALL THIS HAPPEN—ESPECIALLY SINCE GOD'S POWER ALWAYS SHOWS UP BEST IN WEAKNESS. SO HERE I SIT ... GLAD THAT I HAVE NOT BEEN HEALED ON THE OUTSIDE, BUT GLAD THAT I HAVE BEEN HEALED ON THE INSIDE. HEALED FROM MY OWN SELF-CENTERED WANTS AND WISHES.'

Joni Eareckson Tada

Heal me, LORD, and I will be healed;
save me and I will be saved,
for you are the one I praise.

(Jeremiah 17:14)

'CHRISTIANITY DOES NOT PROVIDE THE REASON FOR EACH EXPERIENCE OF PAIN, BUT IT DOES PROVIDE DEEP RESOURCES FOR ACTUALLY FACING SUFFERING WITH HOPE AND COURAGE RATHER THAN BITTERNESS AND DESPAIR.'

Timothy Keller

For he has not despised or scorned
    the suffering of the afflicted one;
he has not hidden his face from him
    but has listened to his cry for help.

(Psalm 22:24)

'HE KNOWS WHEN WE GO INTO THE STORM, HE WATCHES OVER US IN THE STORM, AND HE CAN BRING US OUT OF THE STORM WHEN HIS PURPOSES HAVE BEEN FULFILLED.'

Warren W. Wiersbe

I consider that our present sufferings are not worth comparing with the glory that will be revealed in us.

(Romans 8:18)

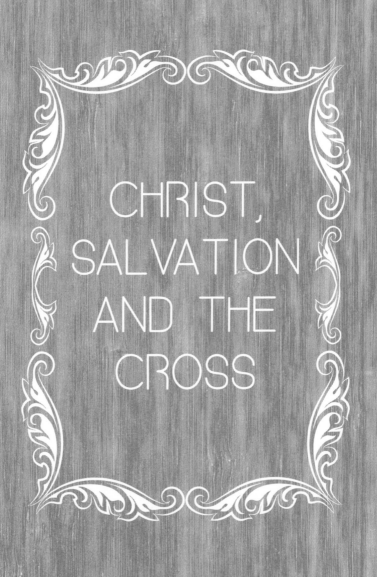

CHRIST,
SALVATION
AND THE
CROSS

'OUR LOVING LORD IS NOT JUST PRESENT, BUT NEARER THAN THE THOUGHT CAN IMAGINE – SO NEAR THAT A WHISPER CAN REACH HIM.'

Amy Carmichael

Come near to God and he will come near to you. Wash your hands, you sinners, and purify your hearts, you double-minded.

(James 4:8)

CHRIST, SALVATION AND THE CROSS

'IF THERE BE GROUND FOR YOU TO TRUST IN YOUR OWN RIGHTEOUSNESS, THEN, ALL THAT CHRIST DID TO PURCHASE SALVATION, AND ALL THAT GOD DID TO PREPARE THE WAY FOR IT IS IN VAIN.'

Jonathan Edwards

Unless the LORD builds the house,
    the builders labor in vain.
Unless the LORD watches over the city,
    the guards stand watch in vain.

(Psalm 127:1)

'CHRIST DID NOT
DIE FOR ANY UPON
CONDITION, IF THEY
DO BELIEVE; BUT HE
DIED FOR ALL GOD'S
ELECT, THAT THEY
SHOULD BELIEVE.'

John Owen

But what does it say? 'The word is
near you; it is in your mouth and
in your heart,' that is, the message
concerning faith that we proclaim.

(Romans 10:8)

'WE ARE NEVER
NEARER CHRIST
THAN WHEN WE
FIND OURSELVES
LOST IN A HOLY
AMAZEMENT AT HIS
UNSPEAKABLE LOVE.'

John Owen

But we do see Jesus, who was made lower than the angels for a little while, now crowned with glory and honor because he suffered death, so that by the grace of God he might taste death for everyone.

(Hebrews 2:9)

'NOT ONLY DO WE KNOW GOD
BY JESUS CHRIST ALONE,
BUT WE KNOW OURSELVES
ONLY BY JESUS CHRIST. WE
KNOW LIFE AND DEATH ONLY
THROUGH JESUS CHRIST.
APART FROM JESUS CHRIST,
WE DO NOT KNOW WHAT IS
OUR LIFE, NOR OUR DEATH,
NOR GOD, NOR OURSELVES.'

Blaise Pascal

Salvation is found in no one else, for there
is no other name under heaven given to
mankind by which we must be saved.

(Acts 4:12)

'IF WE COULD CONDENSE ALL THE TRUTHS OF CHRISTMAS INTO ONLY THREE WORDS, THESE WOULD BE THE WORDS: "GOD WITH US."'

John F. MacArthur

The virgin will conceive and give birth to a son, and they will call him Immanuel (which means 'God with us').

(Matthew 1:23)

'OUTSIDE OF CHRIST, I AM ONLY A SINNER, BUT IN CHRIST, I AM SAVED. OUTSIDE OF CHRIST, I AM EMPTY; IN CHRIST, I AM FULL. OUTSIDE OF CHRIST, I AM WEAK; IN CHRIST, I AM STRONG. OUTSIDE OF CHRIST, I CANNOT; IN CHRIST, I AM MORE THAN ABLE. OUTSIDE OF CHRIST, I HAVE BEEN DEFEATED; IN CHRIST, I AM ALREADY VICTORIOUS. HOW MEANINGFUL ARE THE WORDS, "IN CHRIST".'

Watchman Nee

For I am convinced that neither death nor life, neither angels nor demons, neither the present nor the future, nor any powers, neither height nor depth, nor anything else in all creation, will be able to separate us from the love of God that is in Christ Jesus our Lord.

(Romans 8:38-39)

'THE RESURRECTION OF JESUS CHRIST FROM THE DEAD IS ONE OF THE BEST ATTESTED FACTS ON RECORD. THERE WERE SO MANY WITNESSES TO BEHOLD IT, THAT IF WE DO IN THE LEAST DEGREE RECEIVE THE CREDIBILITY OF MEN'S TESTIMONIES, WE CANNOT AND WE DARE NOT DOUBT THAT JESUS ROSE FROM THE DEAD.'

Charles Spurgeon

… and to wait for his Son from heaven, whom he raised from the dead—Jesus, who rescues us from the coming wrath.

(1 Thessalonians 1:10)

SALVATION
AND
SATISFACTION

'OUR DEEDS ARE NOT THE BASIS OF OUR SALVATION, THEY ARE THE EVIDENCE OF OUR SALVATION. THEY ARE NOT FOUNDATION, THEY ARE DEMONSTRATION.'

John Piper

For it is by grace you have been saved, through faith – and this is not from yourselves, it is the gift of God – not by works, so that no one can boast.

(Ephesians 2:8-9)

'SIN IS WHAT YOU DO WHEN YOUR HEART IS NOT SATISFIED WITH GOD.'

John Piper

To the person who pleases him, God gives wisdom, knowledge and happiness, but to the sinner he gives the task of gathering and storing up wealth to hand it over to the one who pleases God. This too is meaningless, a chasing after the wind.

(Ecclesiastes 2:26)

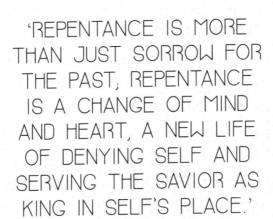

'REPENTANCE IS MORE THAN JUST SORROW FOR THE PAST; REPENTANCE IS A CHANGE OF MIND AND HEART, A NEW LIFE OF DENYING SELF AND SERVING THE SAVIOR AS KING IN SELF'S PLACE.'

J. I. Packer

Repent, then, and turn to God, so that your sins may be wiped out, that times of refreshing may come from the Lord.

(Acts 3:19)

'BEFORE WE CAN BEGIN TO SEE THE CROSS AS SOMETHING DONE FOR US, WE HAVE TO SEE IT AS SOMETHING DONE BY US.'

John Stott

He forgave us all our sins, having canceled the charge of our legal indebtedness, which stood against us and condemned us; he has taken it away, nailing it to the cross.

(Colossians 2:13-14)

SALVATION AND SATISFACTION

'EVERY TIME WE LOOK AT THE CROSS CHRIST SEEMS TO SAY TO US, "I AM HERE BECAUSE OF YOU. IT IS YOUR SIN I AM BEARING, YOUR CURSE I AM SUFFERING, YOUR DEBT I AM PAYING, YOUR DEATH I AM DYING." NOTHING IN HISTORY OR IN THE UNIVERSE CUTS US DOWN TO SIZE LIKE THE CROSS.'

John Stott

And being found in appearance as a man,
he humbled himself
by becoming obedient to death –
even death on a cross!

(Philippians 2:8)

'MAY WE SIT AT THE FOOT OF THE CROSS; AND THERE LEARN WHAT SIN HAS DONE, WHAT JUSTICE HAS DONE, WHAT LOVE HAS DONE.'

John Newton

For the sake of your name, LORD,
forgive my iniquity, though it is great.

(Psalm 25:11)

  SALVATION AND SATISFACTION

'BE ASSURED THAT THERE IS NO SIN YOU HAVE EVER COMMITTED THAT THE BLOOD OF JESUS CHRIST CANNOT CLEANSE.'

Billy Graham

If we confess our sins, he is faithful and just and will forgive us our sins and purify us from all unrighteousness.

(1 John 1:9)

> '**NAILS WERE NOT ENOUGH TO HOLD GOD-AND-MAN NAILED AND FASTENED ON THE CROSS, HAD NOT LOVE HELD HIM THERE.**'

Catherine of Siena

Christ redeemed us from the curse of the law by becoming a curse for us, for it is written: 'Cursed is everyone who is hung on a pole.'

(Galatians 3:13)

'THE AIM AND FINAL END OF ALL MUSIC SHOULD BE NONE OTHER THAN THE GLORY OF GOD AND THE REFRESHMENT OF THE SOUL. IF HEED IS NOT PAID TO THIS, IT IS NOT TRUE MUSIC BUT A DIABOLICAL BAWLING AND TWANGING.'

J. S. Bach

I will sing of your love and justice;
to you, LORD, I will sing praise.

(Psalm 101:1)

'THE TRUTH IS THAT
CONTENTMENT IS NOT FOUND
IN HAVING EVERYTHING WE
THINK WE WANT BUT IN
CHOOSING TO BE SATISFIED
WITH WHAT GOD HAS
ALREADY PROVIDED.'

Nancy Leigh DeMoss

Command those who are rich in this present
world not to be arrogant nor to put their
hope in wealth, which is so uncertain, but to
put their hope in God, who richly provides
us with everything for our enjoyment.

(1 Timothy 6:17)

'GOD IS GOD, YOU ARE BUT
ONE OF HIS CREATURES.
YOUR ONLY JOY IS TO BE
FOUND IN OBEYING HIM,
YOUR TRUE FULFILLMENT IS
TO BE FOUND IN WORSHIPING
HIM, YOUR ONLY WISDOM IS
TO BE FOUND IN TRUSTING
AND KNOWING HIM.'

Sinclair B. Ferguson

You make known to me the path of life;
you will fill me with joy in your presence,
with eternal pleasures at your right hand.

(Psalm 16:11)

'GOD IS MOST GLORIFIED IN US WHEN WE ARE MOST SATISFIED IN HIM.'

John Piper

I will praise you, Lord my God,
with all my heart;
I will glorify your name forever.

(Psalm 86:12)

PRAYER &
THANKFULNESS

'THEY WHO TRULY COME TO GOD FOR MERCY, COME AS BEGGARS, AND NOT AS CREDITORS: THEY COME FOR MERE MERCY, FOR SOVEREIGN GRACE, AND NOT FOR ANYTHING THAT IS DUE'

Jonathan Edwards

He will respond to the prayer of the destitute;
he will not despise their plea.

(Psalm 102:17)

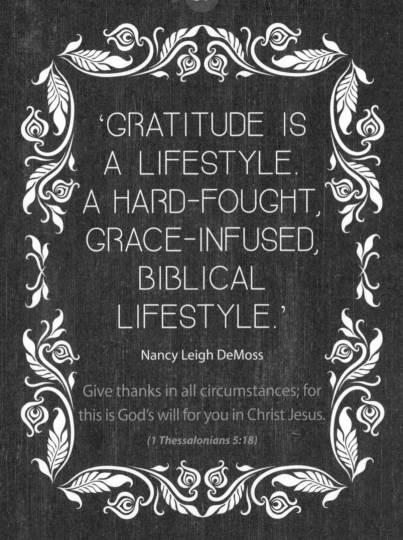

'GRATITUDE IS
A LIFESTYLE.
A HARD-FOUGHT,
GRACE-INFUSED,
BIBLICAL
LIFESTYLE.'

Nancy Leigh DeMoss

Give thanks in all circumstances; for
this is God's will for you in Christ Jesus.

(1 Thessalonians 5:18)

'FOR THE
FAITHFUL,
SPIRIT-FILLED
CHRISTIAN, EVERY
PLACE BECOMES
A PLACE OF
PRAYER.'

John F. MacArthur

Now, my God, may your eyes be
open and your ears attentive to the
prayers offered in this place.

(2 Chronicles 6:40)

'IF WE WOULD TALK LESS AND PRAY MORE ABOUT THEM, THINGS WOULD BE BETTER THAN THEY ARE IN THE WORLD: AT LEAST, WE SHOULD BE BETTER ENABLED TO BEAR THEM.'

John Owen

Therefore let all the faithful pray to you
   while you may be found;
surely the rising of the mighty waters
   will not reach them.

(Psalm 32:6)

'JUST AS THE FIRST SIGN OF LIFE IN AN INFANT WHEN BORN INTO THE WORLD IS THE ACT OF BREATHING, SO THE FIRST ACT OF MEN AND WOMEN WHEN THEY ARE BORN AGAIN IS PRAYING.'

J. C. Ryle

Hear me, LORD, and answer me,
for I am poor and needy.

(Psalm 86:1)

'WE LOOK UPON
PRAYER SIMPLY
AS A MEANS OF
GETTING THINGS FOR
OURSELVES, BUT THE
BIBLICAL PURPOSE OF
PRAYER IS THAT WE
MAY GET TO KNOW
GOD HIMSELF.'

Oswald Chambers

You who answer prayer,
to you all people will come.

(Psalm 65:2)

'SOME PEOPLE THINK GOD DOES NOT LIKE TO BE TROUBLED WITH OUR CONSTANT COMING AND ASKING. THE WAY TO TROUBLE GOD IS NOT TO COME AT ALL.'

Dwight L Moody

But God has surely listened
and has heard my prayer.

(Psalm 66:19)

PRAYER AND THANKFULNESS

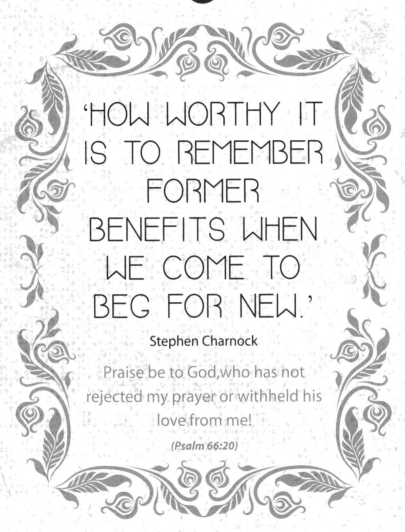

'HOW WORTHY IT IS TO REMEMBER FORMER BENEFITS WHEN WE COME TO BEG FOR NEW.'

Stephen Charnock

Praise be to God, who has not rejected my prayer or withheld his love from me!

(Psalm 66:20)

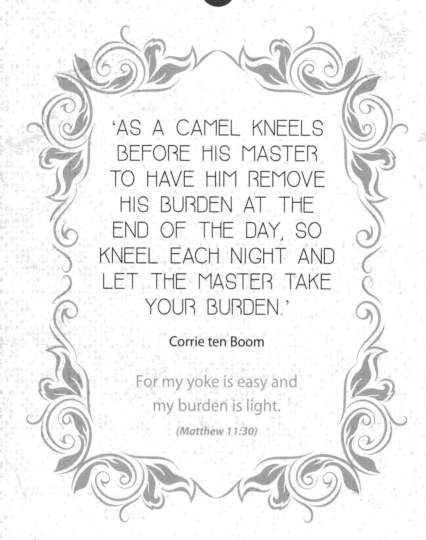

'AS A CAMEL KNEELS
BEFORE HIS MASTER
TO HAVE HIM REMOVE
HIS BURDEN AT THE
END OF THE DAY, SO
KNEEL EACH NIGHT AND
LET THE MASTER TAKE
YOUR BURDEN.'

Corrie ten Boom

For my yoke is easy and
my burden is light.

(Matthew 11:30)

'MAN IS AT HIS GREATEST AND HIGHEST WHEN UPON HIS KNEES HE COMES FACE TO FACE WITH GOD.'

Martyn Lloyd-Jones

But when you pray, go into your room, close the door and pray to your Father, who is unseen. Then your Father, who sees what is done in secret, will reward you.

(Matthew 6:6)

'THOU ART COMING TO A KING, LARGE PETITIONS WITH THEE BRING, FOR HIS GRACE AND POWER ARE SUCH NONE CAN EVER ASK TOO MUCH.'

John Newton

Do not be anxious about anything, but in every situation, by prayer and petition, with thanksgiving, present your requests to God.

(Philippians 4:6)

'TRUE CHRISTIANS CONSIDER THEMSELVES NOT AS SATISFYING SOME RIGOROUS CREDITOR, BUT AS DISCHARGING A DEBT OF GRATITUDE'

William Wilberforce

Let the message of Christ dwell among you richly as you teach and admonish one another with all wisdom through psalms, hymns, and songs from the Spirit, singing to God with gratitude in your hearts.

(Colossians 3:16)

'I THROW MYSELF DOWN
IN MY CHAMBER, AND I
CALL IN AND INVITE GOD
AND HIS ANGELS THITHER;
AND WHEN THEY ARE
THERE, I NEGLECT GOD
AND HIS ANGELS FOR THE
NOISE OF A FLY, FOR THE
RATTLING OF A COACH, FOR
THE WHINING OF A DOOR.'

John Donne

Watch and pray so that you will
not fall into temptation. The spirit
is willing, but the flesh is weak.

(Matthew 26:41)

'THANKS BE TO THEE, O LORD JESUS CHRIST, FOR ALL THE BENEFITS WHICH THOU HAST GIVEN US; FOR ALL THE PAINS AND INSULTS WHICH THOU HAST BORNE FOR US. O MOST MERCIFUL REDEEMER, FRIEND AND BROTHER, MAY WE KNOW THEE MORE CLEARLY, LOVE THEE MORE DEARLY, AND FOLLOW THEE MORE NEARLY; FOR THINE OWN SAKE.'

St. Richard of Chichester

I know that my redeemer lives,
and that in the end he will stand on the earth.

(Job 19:25)

'WHEN THOU PRAYEST, RATHER LET THY HEART BE WITHOUT WORDS THAN THY WORDS BE WITHOUT HEART.'

John Bunyan

In return for my friendship they accuse me, but I am a man of prayer.

(Psalm 109:4)

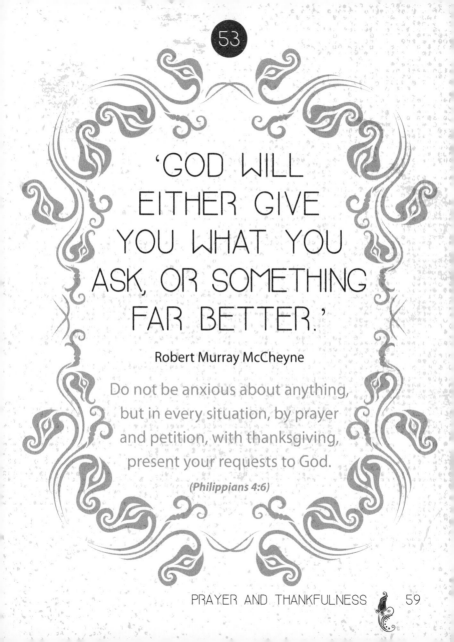

'GOD WILL
EITHER GIVE
YOU WHAT YOU
ASK, OR SOMETHING
FAR BETTER.'

Robert Murray McCheyne

Do not be anxious about anything,
but in every situation, by prayer
and petition, with thanksgiving,
present your requests to God.

(Philippians 4:6)

ETERNITY,
THE FUTURE
AND
CHANGING
OUR WORLD

'LORD, STAMP ETERNITY ON MY EYEBALLS.'

Jonathan Edwards

He has made everything beautiful in its time. He has also set eternity in the human heart; yet no one can fathom what God has done from beginning to end.

(Ecclesiastes 3:11)

'BUT EVEN AN ORDINARY SECRETARY OR A HOUSEWIFE OR A TEENAGER CAN, WITHIN THEIR OWN SMALL WAYS, TURN ON A SMALL LIGHT IN A DARK ROOM.'

Miep Gies

Neither do people light a lamp and put it under a bowl. Instead they put it on its stand, and it gives light to everyone in the house. In the same way, let your light shine before others, that they may see your good deeds and glorify your Father in heaven.

(Matthew 5:15-16)

'EXCEPT A MAN BE BORN AGAIN, HE WILL WISH ONE DAY HE HAD NEVER BEEN BORN AT ALL.'

J. C. Ryle

So must the Son of Man be lifted up, that whoever believes in him may have eternal life.

(John 3:14-15 ESV)

'WE ARE NOT YET WHAT WE SHALL BE, BUT WE ARE GROWING TOWARD IT, THE PROCESS IS NOT YET FINISHED ...'

Martin Luther

Therefore, since we are surrounded by such a great cloud of witnesses, let us throw off everything that hinders and the sin that so easily entangles. And let us run with perseverance the race marked out for us.

(Hebrews 12:1)

'I'M WEARYING TO ESCAPE
INTO THAT GLORIOUS
WORLD, AND TO BE ALWAYS
THERE; NOT SEEING IT
DIMLY THROUGH TEARS, AND
YEARNING FOR IT THROUGH
THE WALLS OF AN ACHING
HEART; BUT REALLY WITH IT,
AND IN IT.'

Emily Bronte

For now we see only a reflection as in a mirror;
then we shall see face to face. Now I know
in part; then I shall know fully, even as I am
fully known.

(1 Corinthians 13:12)

'TRUE GODLINESS DOES NOT TURN MEN OUT OF THE WORLD, BUT ENABLES THEM TO LIVE BETTER IN IT AND EXCITES THEIR ENDEAVORS TO MEND IT.'

William Penn

Even now the one who reaps draws a wage and harvests a crop for eternal life, so that the sower and the reaper may be glad together.

(John 4:36)

ETERNITY, THE FUTURE AND CHANGING OUR WORLD

'ALTHOUGH THE THREADS OF MY LIFE HAVE OFTEN SEEMED KNOTTED, I KNOW, BY FAITH, THAT ON THE OTHER SIDE OF THE EMBROIDERY THERE IS A CROWN.'

Corrie ten Boom

Anyone who loves their life will lose it, while anyone who hates their life in this world will keep it for eternal life.

(John 12:25)

'REJOICE, THAT THE IMMORTAL GOD IS BORN, SO THAT MORTAL MAN MAY LIVE IN ETERNITY.'

Jan Hus

Therefore the Lord himself will give you a sign: The virgin will conceive and give birth to a son, and will call him Immanuel.

(Isaiah 7:14)

'WHEN THE EYES OF THE SOUL LOOKING OUT MEET THE EYES OF GOD LOOKING IN, HEAVEN HAS BEGUN RIGHT HERE ON THIS EARTH.'

A. W. Tozer

Now this is eternal life: that they know you, the only true God, and Jesus Christ, whom you have sent.

(John 17:3)

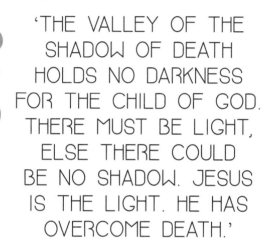

'THE VALLEY OF THE
SHADOW OF DEATH
HOLDS NO DARKNESS
FOR THE CHILD OF GOD.
THERE MUST BE LIGHT,
ELSE THERE COULD
BE NO SHADOW. JESUS
IS THE LIGHT. HE HAS
OVERCOME DEATH.'

Dwight L. Moody

Even though I walk
through the darkest valley,
I will fear no evil, for you are with me;
your rod and your staff, they comfort me.

(Psalm 23:4)

'COVER, LORD, WHAT
HAS BEEN: GOVERN
WHAT SHALL BE.
OH, PERFECT
THAT WHICH THOU
HAST BEGUN,
THAT I SUFFER
NOT SHIPWRECK IN
THE HAVEN.'

Theodore Beza

For the wages of sin is death, but the gift of
God is eternal life in Christ Jesus our Lord.

(Romans 6:23)

'THE BODY OF BENJAMIN FRANKLIN, PRINTER; LIKE THE COVER OF AN OLD BOOK, ITS CONTENTS TORN OUT, AND STRIPPED OF ITS LETTERING AND GILDING, LIES HERE, FOOD FOR WORMS. BUT THE WORK SHALL NOT BE WHOLLY LOST: FOR IT WILL, AS HE BELIEVED, APPEAR ONCE MORE, IN A NEW AND MORE PERFECT EDITION, CORRECTED AND AMENDED BY THE AUTHOR.'

Benjamin Franklin

Whoever sows to please their flesh, from the flesh will reap destruction; whoever sows to please the Spirit, from the Spirit will reap eternal life.

(Galatians 6:8)

'OUR LORD HAS MANY WEAK CHILDREN IN HIS FAMILY, MANY DULL PUPILS IN HIS SCHOOL, MANY RAW SOLDIERS IN HIS ARMY, MANY LAME SHEEP IN HIS FLOCK. YET HE BEARS WITH THEM ALL, AND CASTS NONE AWAY. HAPPY IS THAT CHRISTIAN WHO HAS LEARNED TO DO LIKEWISE WITH HIS BRETHREN.'

J. C. Ryle

All those the Father gives me will come to me, and whoever comes to me I will never drive away.

(John 6:37)

'ALL THE BLESSINGS WE ENJOY ARE DIVINE DEPOSITS, COMMITTED TO OUR TRUST ON THIS CONDITION, THAT THEY SHOULD BE DISPENSED FOR THE BENEFIT OF OUR NEIGHBORS.'

John Calvin

No one should seek their own good, but the good of others.

(1 Corinthians 10:24)

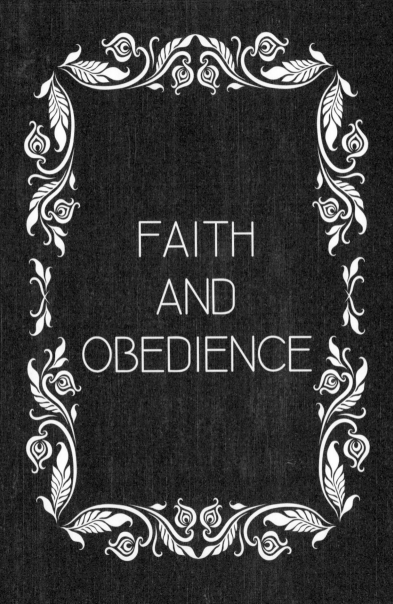

FAITH
AND
OBEDIENCE

'SOMETIMES WE WANT THINGS WE WERE NOT MEANT TO HAVE. BECAUSE HE LOVES US, THE FATHER SAYS NO. FAITH TRUSTS THAT NO. FAITH IS WILLING NOT TO HAVE WHAT GOD IS NOT WILLING TO GIVE.'

Elisabeth Elliot

And we know that in all things God works for the good of those who love him, who have been called according to his purpose.

(Romans 8:28)

'GOD DOESN'T ALWAYS CHANGE THE CIRCUMSTANCES, BUT HE CAN CHANGE US TO MEET THE CIRCUMSTANCES. THAT'S WHAT IT MEANS TO LIVE BY FAITH.'

Warren W. Wiersbe

Yet this I call to mind
    and therefore I have hope:
Because of the LORD's great love
we are not consumed,
    for his compassions never fail.
They are new every morning;
    great is your faithfulness.

(Lamentations 3:21-23)

'FAITH SEES
THE INVISIBLE,
BELIEVES THE
UNBELIEVABLE, AND
RECEIVES THE
IMPOSSIBLE.'

Corrie ten Boom

He replied, 'Because you have so little faith.
Truly I tell you, if you have faith as small as a
mustard seed, you can say to this mountain,
"Move from here to there," and it will move.
Nothing will be impossible for you.'

(Matthew 17:20)

FAITH AND OBEDIENCE

'WHEN OBEDIENCE TO
GOD CONTRADICTS
WHAT I THINK WILL
GIVE ME PLEASURE,
LET ME ASK MYSELF IF
I LOVE HIM.'

Elisabeth Elliot

Be careful to obey all these regulations
I am giving you, so that it may always
go well with you and your children
after you, because you will be doing
what is good and right in the eyes of
the LORD your God.

(Deuteronomy 12:28)

'GOD IS GOD. BECAUSE HE IS GOD, HE IS WORTHY OF MY TRUST AND OBEDIENCE. I WILL FIND REST NOWHERE BUT IN HIS HOLY WILL THAT IS UNSPEAKABLY BEYOND MY LARGEST NOTIONS OF WHAT HE IS UP TO.'

Elisabeth Elliot

But Samuel replied:
'Does the LORD delight in burnt offerings and sacrifices
    as much as in obeying the LORD?
To obey is better than sacrifice,
    and to heed is better than the fat of rams.'

(1 Samuel 15:22)

'I CAN LET CHRIST GRIP ME;
BUT I CANNOT GRIP HIM. I
LOVE TO SIT ON CHRIST'S
KNEE; BUT I CANNOT SET
MY FEET TO THE GROUND,
FOR AFFLICTIONS BRING THE
CRAMP UPON MY FAITH. ALL
I NOW DO, IS, TO HOLD OUT
A LAME FAITH TO CHRIST,
LIKE A BEGGAR HOLDING OUT
A STUMP, INSTEAD OF AN
ARM OR LEG; AND CRY, LORD
JESUS, WORK A MIRACLE.'

Samuel Rutherford

But as for me, I am poor and needy;
   may the Lord think of me.
You are my help and my deliverer;
   you are my God, do not delay.

(Psalm 40:17)

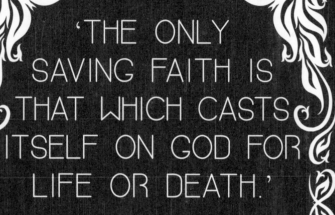

'THE ONLY
SAVING FAITH IS
THAT WHICH CASTS
ITSELF ON GOD FOR
LIFE OR DEATH.'

Martin Luther

But I pray to you, LORD,
   in the time of your favor;
in your great love, O God,
   answer me with your sure salvation.

(Psalm 69:13)

WITNESS
AND
WISDOM

'THE GREATEST
WEAKNESS IN THE
CHURCH TODAY IS THAT
THE SERVANTS OF GOD
KEEP LOOKING OVER
THEIR SHOULDER FOR
THE APPROVAL OF MEN.'

R. C. Sproul

Am I now trying to win the approval
of human beings, or of God? Or am I
trying to please people? If I were still
trying to please people, I would not
be a servant of Christ.

(Galatians 1:10)

'AS THE FEAR OF GOD IS THE BEGINNING OF WISDOM, SO THE DENIAL OF GOD IS THE HEIGHT OF FOOLISHNESS.'

R. C. Sproul

The fear of the LORD is the beginning
of wisdom;
 all who follow his precepts have
 good understanding.
 To him belongs eternal praise.

(Psalm 111:10)

'WHILE THE GOOD
NEWS OF THE GOSPEL
MAY NOT APPEAL TO
EVERYONE, THE BAD NEWS
OF THE GOSPEL STILL
APPLIES TO EVERYONE.'

Matt Chandler

… and to wait for his Son from
heaven, whom he raised from the
dead – Jesus, who rescues us from
the coming wrath.

(1 Thessalonians 1:10)

'INTEGRITY MEANS
THAT IF OUR PRIVATE
LIFE WERE SUDDENLY
EXPOSED, WE'D HAVE NO
REASON TO BE ASHAMED
OR EMBARRASSED.
INTEGRITY MEANS THAT
OUR OUTWARD LIFE IS
CONSISTENT WITH OUR
INNER CONVICTIONS.'

Billy Graham

Whoever walks in integrity walks securely,
but whoever takes crooked paths
will be found out.

(Proverbs 10:9)

'EACH LIFE IS MADE
UP OF MISTAKES AND
LEARNING, WAITING
AND GROWING, PRACTICING
PATIENCE AND BEING
PERSISTENT.'

Billy Graham

But if we hope for what we
do not yet have, we wait for
it patiently.

(Romans 8:25)

'LET YOUR CHRISTIANITY
BE SO UNMISTAKABLE,
YOUR EYE SO SINGLE,
YOUR HEART SO
WHOLE, YOUR WALK SO
STRAIGHTFORWARD,
THAT ALL WHO SEE YOU
MAY HAVE NO DOUBT
WHOSE YOU ARE, AND
WHOM YOU SERVE.'

J. C. Ryle

For we are God's handiwork, created in
Christ Jesus to do good works, which
God prepared in advance for us to do.

(Ephesians 2:10)

'WE MUST GIVE UP
THE VAIN IDEA OF TRYING
TO PLEASE EVERYBODY.
THAT IS IMPOSSIBLE, AND
THE ATTEMPT IS A MERE
WASTE OF TIME. WE
MUST BE CONTENT TO
WALK IN CHRIST'S STEPS,
AND LET THE WORLD SAY
WHAT IT LIKES.'

J. C. Ryle

As a prisoner for the Lord,
then, I urge you to live a life worthy
of the calling you have received.

(Ephesians 4:1)

'LORD, GRANT THAT ANGER
OR OTHER BITTERNESS
DOES NOT REIGN OVER US,
BUT THAT YOUR GRACE,
GENUINE KINDNESS, LOYALTY,
AND EVERY KIND OF
FRIENDLINESS, GENEROSITY,
AND GENTLENESS MAY REIGN
IN US. AMEN'

Martin Luther

But you, man of God, flee from all this,
and pursue righteousness, godliness,
faith, love, endurance and gentleness.

(1 Timothy 6:11)

'THE GREATEST TEST OF CHRISTIANITY IS THE WEAR AND TEAR OF DAILY LIFE; IT IS LIKE THE SHINING OF SILVER: THE MORE IT IS RUBBED THE BRIGHTER IT GROWS.'

Oswald Chambers

For you, God, tested us;
you refined us like silver.

(Psalm 66:10)

'OUR IGNORANCE
OF GOD IS TOO
GREAT, BECAUSE
OUR ESTIMATIONS
OF GOD ARE
TOO LITTLE.'

Stephen Charnock

Are the comforts of God too small
for you, or the word that deals
gently with you?

(Job 15:11 ESV)

'IF THOU WOULDST RULE WELL, THOU MUST RULE FOR GOD, AND TO DO THAT, THOU MUST BE RULED BY HIM... THOSE WHO WILL NOT BE GOVERNED BY GOD WILL BE RULED BY TYRANTS.'

William Penn

You must always be careful to keep the decrees and regulations, the laws and commands he wrote for you. Do not worship other gods.

(2 Kings 17:37)

'WE OUGHT TO
BE LIVING AS IF
JESUS DIED
YESTERDAY, ROSE
THIS MORNING, AND IS
COMING BACK
THIS AFTERNOON.'

Adrian Rogers

But in your hearts revere Christ
as Lord. Always be prepared to
give an answer to everyone who
asks you to give the reason for the
hope that you have. But do this
with gentleness and respect.

(1 Peter 3:15)

'THE GOD YOU
WORSHIP WILL SHAPE
THE VALUES YOU HOLD,
AND THE VALUES YOU
HOLD WILL SHAPE
THE LIFESTYLE THAT
YOU CHOOSE.'

Colin S. Smith

For this very reason, make
every effort to add to your
faith goodness; and to
goodness, knowledge.

(2 Peter 1:5)

'GOING TO CHURCH DOESN'T MAKE YOU A CHRISTIAN, ANY MORE THAN GOING TO A GARAGE MAKES YOU AN AUTOMOBILE.'

Billy Sunday

They claim to know God, but by their actions they deny him. They are detestable, disobedient and unfit for doing anything good.

(Titus 1:16)

THE
CREATOR,
CREATION
AND US

'IF GOD IS THE CREATOR OF THE ENTIRE UNIVERSE, THEN IT MUST FOLLOW THAT HE IS THE LORD OF THE WHOLE UNIVERSE. NO PART OF THE WORLD IS OUTSIDE OF HIS LORDSHIP. THAT MEANS THAT NO PART OF MY LIFE MUST BE OUTSIDE OF HIS LORDSHIP.'

R. C. Sproul

There is one body and one Spirit, just as you were called to one hope when you were called; one Lord, one faith, one baptism; one God and Father of all, who is over all and through all and in all.

(Ephesians 4:4-5)

90

'WE CAN NEVER
GRASP THE
EXTENT OF OUR
DEPRAVITY UNTIL
WE RECOGNIZE
THE EXCELLENCIES
OF OUR CREATED
DIGNITY'

Matt Chandler

Good and upright is the LORD;
therefore he instructs sinners in his ways.

(Psalm 25:8)

91

'I NEVER GET TIRED OF THE BLUE SKY.'

Vincent Van Gogh

The heavens declare the glory of God; the skies proclaim the work of his hands.

(Psalm 19:1)

'LIVING BECOMES AN
AWESOME BUSINESS WHEN
YOU REALIZE THAT YOU
SPEND EVERY MOMENT OF
YOUR LIFE IN THE SIGHT AND
COMPANY OF AN OMNISCIENT,
OMNIPRESENT CREATOR.'

J. I. Packer

Do you not know?
   Have you not heard?
The LORD is the everlasting God,
   the Creator of the ends of the earth.
He will not grow tired or weary,
   and his understanding no one
can fathom.

(Isaiah 40:28)

'I AM NOT ASKING WHETHER YOU KNOW THINGS ABOUT HIM BUT DO YOU KNOW GOD, ARE YOU ENJOYING GOD, IS GOD THE CENTRE OF YOUR LIFE, THE SOUL OF YOUR BEING, THE SOURCE OF YOUR GREATEST JOY? HE IS MEANT TO BE.'

Martyn Lloyd-Jones

Be still, and know that I am God;
I will be exalted among the nations,
I will be exalted in the earth.

(Psalm 46:10)

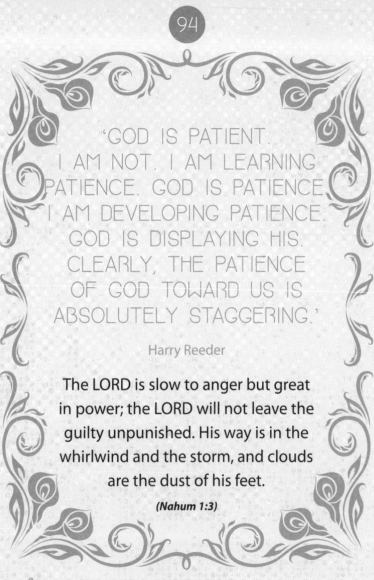

'GOD IS PATIENT.
I AM NOT. I AM LEARNING
PATIENCE. GOD IS PATIENCE.
I AM DEVELOPING PATIENCE.
GOD IS DISPLAYING HIS.
CLEARLY, THE PATIENCE
OF GOD TOWARD US IS
ABSOLUTELY STAGGERING.'

Harry Reeder

The LORD is slow to anger but great
in power; the LORD will not leave the
guilty unpunished. His way is in the
whirlwind and the storm, and clouds
are the dust of his feet.

(Nahum 1:3)

GOD'S WORD, LOVE AND ACTION

'THE BIBLE IS A REMARKABLE FOUNTAIN: THE MORE ONE DRAWS AND DRINKS OF IT, THE MORE IT STIMULATES THIRST.'

Martin Luther

For with you is the fountain of life;
in your light we see light.

(Psalm 36:9)

'THE BIBLE SAYS
THAT OUR REAL
PROBLEM IS THAT
EVERY ONE OF
US IS BUILDING
OUR IDENTITY
ON SOMETHING
BESIDES JESUS.'

Timothy Keller

Fear the LORD your God and serve him. Hold
fast to him and take your oaths in his name.

(Deuteronomy 10:20)

'THOUGH TROUBLES ASSAIL AND DANGERS AFFRIGHT, THOUGH FRIENDS SHOULD ALL FAIL AND FOES ALL UNITE; YET ONE THING SECURES US, WHATEVER BETIDE, THE SCRIPTURE ASSURES US, THE LORD WILL PROVIDE.'

John Newton

And my God will meet all your needs according to the riches of his glory in Christ Jesus.

(Philippians 4:19)

98

'THE HOLY
SCRIPTURES ARE
OUR LETTERS
FROM HOME.'

St. Augustine

Then the LORD said to Moses,
'Write down these words, for in
accordance with these words I
have made a covenant with you
and with Israel.'

(Exodus 34:27)

'IF I SIT NEXT TO A MADMAN AS HE DRIVES A CAR INTO A GROUP OF INNOCENT BYSTANDERS, I CAN'T, AS A CHRISTIAN, SIMPLY WAIT FOR THE CATASTROPHE, THEN COMFORT THE WOUNDED AND BURY THE DEAD. I MUST TRY TO WRESTLE THE STEERING WHEEL OUT OF THE HANDS OF THE DRIVER.'

Dietrich Bonhoeffer

Do not keep talking so proudly
   or let your mouth speak such arrogance,
for the LORD is a God who knows,
   and by him deeds are weighed.

(1 Samuel 2:3)

'I THINK ONE'S FEELINGS WASTE THEMSELVES IN WORDS; THEY OUGHT ALL TO BE DISTILLED INTO ACTIONS WHICH BRING RESULTS.'

Florence Nightingale

Be devoted to one another in love. Honor one another above yourselves.

(Romans 12:10)

101

'I LOVE MY GOD, BUT WITH
NO LOVE OF MINE
FOR I HAVE NONE TO GIVE;
I LOVE THEE, LORD, BUT ALL
THAT LOVE IS THINE,
FOR BY THY LIFE I LIVE.
I AM AS NOTHING, AND
REJOICE TO BE
EMPTIED AND LOST AND
SWALLOWED UP IN THEE.'

Mme. Guyon

We love because he first loved us.

(1 John 4:19)

END
NOTES

WORK, CALLING, LIFE

1. J.R.R. Tolkien, *The Lord of the Rings: One Volume* (2012), Houghton Mifflin Harcourt

2. J. I. Packer, *Rediscovering Holiness* (2009), Baker Books

3. William Wilberforce, quoted in *The Life of William Wilberforce* (1839), Robert Isaac Wilberforce and Samuel Wilberforce, Perkins

GOD, HIS WILL AND OUR HOLINESS

4. Dietrich Bonhoeffer , *Life Together* (2015), SCM Press

5. Joni Eareckson Tada, *Secret Strength: For Those Who Search* (2011), Multnomah

6. Jonathan Edwards, *The Philosophy of Jonathan Edwards* (2009), Steven Daniel, Wipf and Stock Publishers

7. Hudson Taylor, quoted in Hudson Taylor's *Spiritual Secret* (1990), F Howard Taylor, Discovery House

8.   Jonathan Edwards, *The Works of President Edwards* (1806)

9.   John Owen, *The Mortification of Sin in Believers* (1842)

SUFFERING AND TRUST

10.   Amy Carmichael, *Candles in the Dark* (2010), CLC Publications

11.   Elisabeth Elliot, *Taking Flight* (1999), Baker Publishing Group

12.   Corrie ten Boom, *Jesus is Victor* (1985), Fleming H Revell Company

13.   J. I. Packer, *In God's Presence* (2000), Shaw

14.   John Newton, *The Works of the Rev. John Newton* (1839)

15.   Joni Eareckson Tada, *A Place of Healing* (2010), David C Cook

16.   Timothy Keller, *The Reason for God* (2008), Penguin

17.   Warren W. Wiersbe, *Looking Up When Life Gets You Down* (2012), Baker Books

CHRIST, SALVATION
AND THE CROSS

18. Amy Carmichael, *Candles in the Dark* (2010), CLC Publications

19. Jonathan Edwards, *History of Redemption* (1793)

20. John Owen, *The Works of John Owen* (1852), Johnstone and Hunter

21. John Owen, *An Exposition of the Epistle to the Hebrews* (1790)

22. Blaise Pascal, *Pascal's Pensees* (2013), Simon and Schuster

23. John F. MacArthur, *Truth for Today* (2006), Thomas Nelson Inc

24. Watchman Nee, *Secrets to Spiritual Power* (1999), Whitaker House

25. Charles Spurgeon, *The Complete Works of C. H. Spurgeon, Volume 2* (2015), Delmarva Publications, Inc.

SALVATION AND SATISFACTION

26. John Piper, *Future Grace* (2012), Multnomah

27. John Piper, *Future Grace* (2012), Multnomah

28. J. I. Packer, *Evangelism and the Sovereignty of God* (2008), IVP

29. John Stott, *The Cross* (2009), IVP

30. John Stott, *The Message of Galatians* (2014), IVP

31. John Newton, *One Hundred and Twenty Nine Letters...* (1847)

32. Billy Graham, *Billy Graham in Quotes* (2011), Thomas Nelson Inc

33. Attributed to Catherine of Siena (1347-1380)

34. Attributed to J. S. Bach (1685-1750)

35. Nancy Leigh DeMoss, *Lies Women Believe* (2007), Moody Publishers

36. Sinclair B. Ferguson, *A Heart for God* (1985), NavPress Publishing Group

37. John Piper, *For Your Joy* (2005), Desiring God

PRAYER AND THANKFULNESS

38. Jonathan Edwards, *Sermons of Jonathan Edwards* (2005), Hendrickson Publishers

39. Nancy Leigh DeMoss, *Choosing Gratitude: Your Journey to Joy* (2009), Moody Publishers

40. John F. MacArthur, *Ephesians MacArthur New Testament Commentary* (1986), Moody Publishers

41. John Owen, *The Works of John Owen* (1852)

42. J. C. Ryle, *A Call to Prayer* (2015), Editora Dracaena

43. Oswald Chambers, *My Utmost for His Highest* (2010), Discovery House

44. Dwight L. Moody, *Prevailing Prayer* (1987), Moody Publishers

45. Stephen Charnock, *Discourses Upon the Existence and Attributes of God* (1874)

46. Corrie ten Boom, *Jesus is Victor* (1985), Fleming H Revell Company

47. Martyn Lloyd-Jones, *Studies in the Sermon on the Mount* (1961), IVP

48. John Newton, *Olney Hymns* (1856)

49. William Wilberforce, *A Practical View of Christianity* (2006), Hendrickson Publishers

50. John Donne, 'Sermon LXXX: Preached at the funeral of Sir William Cokayne, December 12, 1626' *The Works of John Donne Volume 3* (1640)

51. Attributed to St. Richard of Chichester (1197-1253)

52. Attributed to John Bunyan, from *A Puritan Golden Treasury*, Dr. I. D. E. Thomas (2007), Banner of Truth

53. Robert Murray McCheyne, quoted in *Memoir and remains of the rev. Robert Murray M'Cheyne, minister of St. Peter's church, Dundee* (1844), Andrew Alexander Bonar

ETERNITY, THE FUTURE AND CHANGING OUR WORLD

54. Attributed to Jonathan Edwards (1703-1758)

55. Miep Gies, *Anne Frank Remembered* (2009), Pocket Books

56. J. C. Ryle, *Bible commentary – The gospel of Matthew* (2015), Editora Dracaena

57. Martin Luther, *Works of Martin Luther* (1943), General Books LLC

58. Emily Bronte, *The Bronte Sisters* (2009), Penguin

59. William Penn, *No Cross, No Crown* (2001), Destiny Image Publishers

60. Corrie ten Boom, *Tramp for the Lord* (1974), CLC Publications

61. Attributed to Jan Hus (1372-1415)

62. A. W. Tozer, *The Pursuit of God* (1948)

63. Dwight L Moody, *Prevailing Prayer* (1884), Moody Publishers

64. Theodore Beza, his last words, quoted in *The Last Hours of Eminent Christians* (1829), Henry Clissold, Rivingtons

65. Benjamin Franklin, inscribed on his tombstone

66. J. C. Ryle, *Bible commentary – The gospel of John* (2015), Editora Dracaena

67. John Calvin, *The Institutes of the Christian Religion* (1536)

FAITH AND OBEDIENCE

68. Elisabeth Elliot, *A Lamp for My Feet* (1987), Vine Books

69. Warren W. Wiersbe, *Be Amazed* (1996), David C Cook

70. Corrie ten Boom, *Jesus is Victor* (1985), Fleming H Revell Company

71. Elisabeth Elliot, *Passion and Purity* (2002), Revell

72. Elisabeth Elliot, *Gates of Splendor* (1996), Guild America Books

73. Samuel Rutherford (1600-1661) letter (1637)

74. Martin Luther, quoted in *A Treasury of Sermon Illustrations* (1950), Charles Langworthy Wallis, Abingdon-Cokesbury Press

WITNESS AND WISDOM

75. R. C. Sproul, Twitter post on Feb 16, 2016

76. R. C. Sproul, *Essential Truths of the Christian Faith* (2011), Tyndale House Publishers, Inc.

77. Matt Chandler, Michael Snetzer, *Recovering Redemption* (2014), B&H Publishing Group

78. Billy Graham, *The Journey* (2007), Thomas Nelson Inc

79. Billy Graham, *Nearing Home* (2013), Thomas Nelson Inc

80. J. C. Ryle, *Old Paths* (2015), Ravenio Books

81. J. C. Ryle, *Bible Commentary – The Gospel of Luke* (2015), Editora Dracaena

82. Martin Luther, *Jesus, Remember Me* (1998), Augsburg Books

83. Oswald Chambers, *Our Brilliant Heritage* (2015), Discovery House

84. Stephen Charnock, *The Works of the Late Rev. Stephen Charnock* (1815)

85. William Penn, 'Letter to Peter the Great, the Czar of Russia, on July 02, 1698', quoted in *The Life of William Penn* (1852), Samuel M. Janney, Friends' Book Association

86. Adrian Rogers, *Unveiling the End Times in Our Time* (2013), B&H Publishing Group

87. Colin S. Smith, *Momentum* (2016), Moody Publishers

88. Billy Sunday, quoted in *Billy Sunday: The Man and His Message* (1914), William T. Ellis, L. T. Myers

THE CREATOR, CREATION AND US

89. R. C. Sproul, *The Holiness of God* (2013), Tyndale House Publishers, Inc.

90. Matt Chandler, Michael Snetzer, *Recovering Redemption* (2014), B&H Publishing Group

91. Vincent Van Gogh, *Complete Letters* (1959)

92. J. I. Packer, *Knowing God Devotional Journal: A One-Year Guide* (2009), IVP

93. Martyn Lloyd-Jones, *Spiritual Depression: Its Causes and Cures* (2016), Zondervan

94. Harry Reeder, 'The Patience of God', First published in Tabletalk Magazine (2004), Ligonier Ministries)

GOD'S WORD, LOVE AND ACTION

95. Martin Luther, *What Luther says: an anthology* (1959), Concordia

96. Timothy Keller, *Jesus the King* (2013) Penguin

97. John Newton (1725-1807), *The Works of the Rev. John Newton* (1839)

98. Attributed to St. Augustine of Hippo

99. Attributed to Dietrich Bonhoeffer (1906-1945)

100. Florence Nightingale, *Suggestions for Thought by Florence Nightingale* (1994), University of Pennsylvania Press

101. Jean Marie Guyon, 'Adoration' https://www.all-creatures.org/poetry/adoration.html Last accessed 14 Feb 2019